Using Your Church Web Site for Evangelism

Vernon Blackmore

Internet Consultant

GROVE BOOKS LIMITED
RIDLEY HALL RD   CAMBRIDGE   CB3 9HU

Contents

Acknowledgements

I owe thanks to Rosie Nixson for inviting me to contribute this material and to her colleagues on the Grove Evangelism group for their wise and helpful suggestions. SGC Design also offered very helpful comments.

The Cover Illustration is by Peter Ashton

Church Army and the Grove Evangelism Series

Church Army has over 350 evangelists working in five areas of focus, at the cutting edge of evangelism in the UK. It co-sponsors the publication of the Grove Evangelism Series as part of its aim of stimulating discussion about evangelism strategies, and sharing its experience of front-line evangelism.

Further details about Church Army are available from:
Church Army, Independents Road, Blackheath, London SE3 9LG.
Telephone: 020 8318 1226. Fax: 020 8318 5258.
Registered charity number: 226226

First Impression February 2001
ISSN 1367-0840
ISBN 1 85174 457 6

1
Introduction

Introducing Dora Bletchley

This book is about using local church web sites *evangelistically*. It is not about using internet tools (both web and e-mail) for church administration and communication. Nor is it about the wider agenda of evangelism and the internet as Christians become involved with this new medium. Of course there is a need for Christians as they use e-mail and engage with others in newsgroups, web-based discussion forums, chat rooms or whatever to be Christ-centred. The issues here are similar to those in personal witness at work or 'gossiping the gospel' to neighbours and friends. But it is not the focus of this book. Our focus is how we can use church web sites to proclaim the Good News.

When I was a young(er) editor at Lion Publishing I was introduced to Dora Bletchley who read all of Lion's books. A survey had once pronounced that Dora was the most common woman's name and Bletchley the most typical of English towns. So this fictitious woman was created to represent a typical reader and all our editing was done with her in mind.

This theme will recur throughout this booklet because as we create local church web sites we will need to remember our audience. But here I mention it in order to discuss *this* book. The subject may be using the web evangelistically, but for whom exactly is it written?

The content bridges both technology and evangelism. As a reader you may be a passionate and experienced evangelist. Perhaps you want to see what this latest medium has to offer. Or you could be a techno-freak with web server bits all over your lounge carpet. Maybe you are wondering how you can use your skills in the service of the local church. You could be a mixture of both. Certainly this book is a mixture, with the inevitable dangers of explaining what is, to some, old hat. Please skip over the sections that cover well-known ground.

My own preference is to make this a practical book, but it is not a primer on web design software. I hope ministers, evangelism committees and the church's web team (now there is a thought for some!) will use this book as a means of reviewing the issues and deciding on where the web fits into their church's wider mission strategy. Its main focus is on communication not technology.

From Athens to AOL

When the apostle Paul talked about Christ in Athens, he was asked to explain his teaching at the Areopagus—the city square where, under the great colonnaded porticos built by foreign kings and benefactors, the people met to debate the latest religious and philosophical views. Paul was used to public speaking, but here the context was very different to a Jewish synagogue. Luke in Acts 17 records the bare bones of what was said. The apostle spoke of the central truths of the gospel but used the ideas and interests of Athenians as a backdrop. The local culture and local communication methods formed the context in which he spoke.

Why was Paul in Athens? Scholars have highlighted how Paul moved from one strategic town to another, following the Roman roads which acted as conduits for news. Paul hoped the same roads would carry the Good News too. The communication centres of his day were the natural places for his proclamation. Not only did these towns guarantee ready audiences, but they would be audiences which would disperse all over the Roman Empire. Acts records instances where Paul was clearly guided by the Spirit to select a location. But there are just as many instances where the decision appears to have rested on 'common sense.'

The Bible is clear about our Great Commission. But it leaves it to us to determine the communication media most suitable in any age. Today's America On Line and St Paul's Athens are many centuries and cultures apart. The evangelist Billy Graham has written in his biography, 'The message of the gospel never changes—and for good reason: God never changes, and neither does our basic spiritual need nor his answer to that need. But the methods of presenting that message do change—and in fact must change if we are to keep pace with a changing world.'

Extras on the Web

This book could be full of links to web resources, both secular and Christian. However, these links would quickly date and new resources would be impossible to add. But this is where the web itself is a more helpful publishing medium than a book. I have set up a companion site to this booklet at **http://www.webevangelism.net**. On the site is additional information. I, and I hope in due course you, can place additional material and links to other relevant sites.

4

2
Medium and the Message

The medium through which we express the Good News inevitably influences what we can say and the manner in which we 'speak.' A famous ballerina was once asked what one of her dances was saying. 'If I could have said it,' she retorted, 'I would never have danced it.' Music can convey deep emotion and evoke long-lasting associations. But it is not much good at reasoned argument. A book can convince the mind, yet its very structure of page following page can be intimidating to those not trained to use it. As I browse the web some issues about this particular medium surface.

It is a Library and Not a Book

For sheer convenience and ease of use, the book and magazine are ideal. Computer monitors are not as good at displaying text. Just as the TV never fully replaced the theatre, so the web will not replace books. But the web does allow a person to use text in new ways. The links, which are at the heart of the web, allow you to relate items together in creative ways.

A book traps you within itself. You have to rise from your comfortable chair to fetch another book to look up a word or a cross-reference. On the web, the next resource is only a click away. In the user's mind, it is one vast landscape of information with no border guards to restrict travel. Searching the web can be a journey through many different sources from many different cultures.

It is All Fragmented

Using a web site is like scanning the magazine table at your doctor's surgery. You pick through the pile, hoping for something to catch your eye. You read a sentence or two and if the point is not made within a few sentences, the magazine is discarded. You read through old *Reader's Digests* hunting out the jokes at the end of the articles. Maybe as you do so you will fasten on to something longer. Maybe you will not.

Just so with the web. People are seldom prepared to follow a lengthy argument as they click from one screen to the next. There are too many distractions, too many possibilities. Information is broken into small segments. People expect to be able to start and stop anywhere.

It is Information More Than Entertainment

The web offers a vast pool of information. There are entertainment sites, where the focus is playing games, listening to music or watching videos. But at present they are in the minority. Although the technology offers a responsive medium that is good for entertainment, it is still difficult and expensive to implement. The current slow connection speeds mean the web is not suited to high-speed action games or video. This will change. As our connections become faster, so will the action on the web. But at the moment the majority of sites present information.

Connecting to the web can be expensive. In the UK we are used to paying for web access by the minute as the meters on our telephone accounts spin on relentlessly. This is changing. An increasingly common approach is to pay a fixed monthly charge regardless of the hours spent on-line. This brings a new attitude. The expense is just the same whether you surf for five minutes or swim for ninety, so people can be less hurried in their hunt for information, entertainment or the best buy. Once you have caught the bus into town you might as well window shop for a while.

It is Responsive Not Static
A web site can offer many opportunities for interaction. The route a person navigates through your site is entirely up to him or her. The medium encourages jumping from one point to another rather than the linear approach needed to read a book.

It is also responsive in another way. A well-designed site will give its readers opportunities to respond to the creator or organizers of the site. Any marketing person will say that selling involves both presentation and allowing people to respond in easy ways. The most a magazine can offer is a 'just clip out the coupon' offer. On the web, a response box inviting your comment or suggesting you leave your e-mail address can be placed alongside articles. It can be so simple to make a response. This opens the opportunity to develop a continuing link with the reader.

With young people internet 'chat rooms' are very popular. Here you can converse with another individual or as a group. At present all the words have to be typed (which enhances anonymity but limits conversation speed), but in future they will be spoken. This may be exciting stuff now, but it will certainly be eclipsed by later technologies. Who knows how future computers will allow us to interact. Maybe future internet shopping will be more like a trip down to the supermarket, with a virtual world we can explore and within which we can meet. Whatever the future, this medium allows interaction in a way that books, radio and television can only do falteringly.

It is All Pick 'n' Mix
Graham Cray has highlighted how today's culture is happy to stitch together its beliefs from a patchwork of remnants from the old beliefs along with some fabrics from the new (see his Grove booklet P 76 *Postmodern Culture and Youth Discipleship* or *The Gospel and Tomorrow's Culture*, CPAS). Not surprisingly people find the blanket cosy as it is made to fit them personally. It is the inevitable result of our shrinking world. We live in a racially and culturally mixed society, we watch TV from around the world and we holiday hundreds of miles away from home. The world wide web only accentuates this. On the web you have access to millions of pages, each able to present its own view. The very phrase 'surf the

web' coveys it. No one gets wet, no one gets drowned—we quickly skim over the surface.

In book publishing it requires a bit of skill to become an author. Printing is expensive and publishers cannot risk their money publishing anything and everything. On the web anyone can have their 15Mb of fame. In the context of so many different voices the notion of authoritative truth takes a real battering. Your church may produce a brilliant web site, but its message appears as but one of many. If you start proclaiming unique truth you stand the danger of looking cranky.

It is Cheap and Can Be Nasty

Some of the larger sites cost millions of pounds/dollars/yen to create. They are big budget affairs. At the other end of the spectrum an individual can use free software to publish pages using a free web server. We have all cringed at poorly acted church drama, yet we allow tasteless and poorly constructed web pages to represent our churches. It is partly because it can be done so easily ('I have a computer, I can put up a web page,' says the enthusiast) and partly because the technology can appear bewildering ('Fine—I don't understand these things' comes the minister's response). It is also out of sight. Unless you browse the web your church's web site is invisible whereas a decrepit notice board outside the church cries out every Sunday for a new coat of paint.

It is Here to Stay

We are at the beginning of a revolution, not its end. Think back to the Reformation. Those early printing presses were so rudimentary compared with today's multi-page, multi-colour, multi-everything machines. The Reformation church used that early technology to spread their message (or propaganda, depending on your view). The printing presses have been rolling ever since.

In a similar way, the internet will increasingly permeate our lives. One day it will disappear. When you get into work, no one asks you if you connected to your 'ESP' earlier that morning. Your ESP is your Electricity Service Provider, but this jargon is forgotten as everyone assumes your house is wired for electricity. Within minutes of getting out of bed, you have 'logged on' half a dozen times to your chosen ESP as you turn on the radio, the light, the shower, the toaster…Your focus is on the application ('making breakfast') rather than the underlying technology that delivers electrical energy.

Give it a few more years and the internet will be everywhere. It will be the transport mechanism for our information, entertainment and communication. In the future, talking about the technology rather than the communication itself will appear rather quaint.

It Will Change Our Theology

Technology always influences the way we think and the categories and metaphors we use to express ourselves. The advent of mass-produced books brought with it a theology that talked of The Book. An understanding of mechanics

(Newton *et alia*) spawned deism and belief in a God who created the world like a watch. The successful march of Victorian industrialization introduced concepts of history and a rejection of miracles. The disillusionment in science these last forty years has gone hand in hand with a rejuvenation in belief in miracles and an interest in spiritual phenomena. What will the internet bring? What new ways of picturing God will it unlock? Where 'book' conveys once-given and one-way revelation, the web implies ever-changing and two-way contact. The Greeks used *logos* to convey all knowledge. Maybe—just maybe—scholars at the end of this century will translate St John as '...the web became flesh and dwelt among us.'

The Heart of the Matter

Will the church be present as a voice within this new medium? You may rightly question the value of setting up a church web site. I certainly do not place it at the top of a church's mission agenda. What is vital is that local churches learn how to use the technology *now* so that they are in a position to be effective when it does count. Remember how your second *Alpha* course went more smoothly than the first? It will take you two years to learn how to build an effective web site. You can master the current technology in a matter of weeks, but this is not the learning to which I am referring. The difficult questions are all the communication ones: Who uses your church web site? How do you create good content? What sorts of people make the best web team members? How does it relate to your other evangelistic ministries? If we learn these lessons today while only a handful are viewing our pages, maybe we will be ready for when it really does matter.

There is one thing I am convinced about. The web is only a support to the church's evangelism, never its heart. Our gospel is all about the incarnation, about God becoming human so that he 'dwelt with us.' Report after report has highlighted that it is the witness of involved *people* who make the difference. John Finney's *People Finding Faith* makes it clear that very few are converted by reading evangelistic books. Surfing the web will be no different.

The biography of William Golding (of *Lord of the Flies* fame) makes sad reading for evangelists. The young William was enthralled by the mystery of religion, yet suffered at the hands of a tyrannical RE teacher. In contrast, he was bored with the barrenness of a materialist, scientific world-view, yet was loved by a physics teacher who preached it. In the end, totally against his natural inclination, he chose a materialist view. He rejected God because one teacher scolded while another loved. 'People form the walls of your rooms,' he wrote, 'not philosophies.'

It is people who will win others for Christ. Hesitant, uncertain, not fully-sorted-out people. And they will need support. For this reason churches run guest services, family services, *Alpha* groups and so on. The materials and methods are there to support the personal witness, never to replace it. Creating a web site for your local church can be a support for the mission of the church. It can make people aware of the church's existence, tell them how to get to it, introduce some of the groups within the church etc. But it is very unlikely to convince and convert.

3
Some Lessons from St Mark's

St Mark's is a real, active church in the centre of England. The congregations are not huge nor is there a vast reservoir of people or financial resources. In 1999 they began using e-mail for their church office and decided that a web site was a good idea. The technical creator was a young person in the congregation while the overall control was in the hands of two older members. They made a team of three. The minister reviewed the pages, but largely left them to get on with it.

Let us look at the starting page of their site as it was just before this book was published. Like a story in a sermon, we can use it to highlight some important points.

Looking at the Site

The site has a lot going for it. The colours are good, the design is clean and the navigation is straightforward. A few pictures could make it look more interesting but (looking at it from another angle) there are no large images to slow things down. Perhaps the young person's enthusiasm for the technology shines through. There is a scrolling message at the bottom of the screen, a hit counter which only shows how infrequently the site is accessed, and some background images which have an infuriating habit of making the text unreadable. But as church sites go, the interface is attractive and clear.

But what is the site trying to do? For whom is it designed?

After a brief welcome, the home page launches into the mission of the church. For the saints this is well known as every pew on Sunday has a mission card within it. No church member is going to let his or her mouse nibble long on this screen. For those outside the church, it is pretty meaningless and dotted with jargon such as 'making disciples.' It offers a 'welcome,' but does not really engage in small talk to help the stranger.

Tracing the history of the site's creation, it appears the material came from the Welcome Pack given to newcomers to the church. But is material designed for those who are brave enough to come into the church building the right approach for a public web site?

Why Do People Visit a Church Web Site?

Why do people visit a church's web site? I do not know of any surveys to guide us and the answer will vary from church to church. Here is my list.

- Your regular congregation will visit the site to look up news, past sermons and the church diary. They will need to know the telephone number of the churchwarden and which Sunday is Family Service.
- Young people associated with the church may want to use a part of the church site as their own. Here they can show off their camp pictures and communicate within the group.
- Parents, both within and without the church, may be looking for information on the Brownies and other church-affiliated groups.
- New people coming into the area will be looking out for churches. They may see a web site as a sign of a positive church, much like newcomers assess a church notice board before stepping inside. They will need to know what the church does, and when.
- Complete outsiders may need information such as how to arrange a baptism or a wedding.
- Enthusiasts of religious architecture may want to know about your rood screen, or whatever. Bell ringers may want to find out about the bells.
- No one will be asking 'how do I become a Christian' and need to find an answer on the web from their local church.

Church web sites fall into two heaps: those that support the saints and those that try to convert the confused. There is often not enough material in the middle. As with all evangelism, the starting point is to answer people's needs. We all know the lessons of John 4 where Jesus talked about the woman's immediate needs before confronting her with truth.

Comments on the St Mark's Site

If we take the above points with respect to the St Mark's site, how well does their home page fare?

- The regular congregation will skip over the home page. They have read it all before, many, many times.
- There are no youth pages yet and a curious young person is offered no hints on the home page about the active youth work in the church.
- Parents looking for information on affiliated groups will be disappointed. The home page makes no reference to it. Within the site there is a simple list of which groups meet on which evening, but the only contact number is for the youth worker.
- New people to the area, if they are Christians, may be encouraged to find a church with a positive mission. But they will quickly want to move off the first page to find information they need. Are there house groups? Is there a Sunday school? Here the site does work as there is information on these matters and a contact phone number for the minister.
- Complete outsiders will be lost. How do they find out about weddings or baptisms? As they dig deeper into the site, they can find the time of the services, the phone number of the minister and a wealth of stuff on missionary work overseas, but no help at all for *their* questions.
- St Mark's was designed by Sir George Gilbert Scott the younger and built in 1879. It is not the UK's finest church, but some do visit it to see its architecture and there is some fine stained glass by Kemp in the chancel. The web site makes no mention of this.
- There is no guidance at all on what it means to be a Christian today to catch a visitor's eye.

Just Fill in the Form

The other pages on the St Mark's web site mention the times of the services and give the minister's phone number. Basic information on the services is all there. But what if you need to know more? The next step offered is to phone the church office. There are no easy ways to respond such as typing your question directly on to the site and hitting a *Send* button. True, the home page mentions an e-mail address, and this can call the user's e-mail software (via a standard link). But many computers are not set up to handle this, so this link may fail. A response form on the page is easier for the user and far, far more reliable.

The Saints Come Marching In

There is nothing wrong in recognizing that the church's web site is primarily a notice board for the faithful. For a busy church (or a cell-like church with no central building or regular gathering) it may be right to use the web site's home page as a place to put the latest news—a virtual notice sheet. But as with many things in the church, we may have to forgo our convenience and break out of our club mentality to use our resources for those outside the church and not within it. A church's home page on the web must surely focus on the needs of others. The congregation can quickly learn to click on a link to find their church news— and, anyway, they can bookmark the news page in their browser. They need never see the home page again! But for those outside the church, the home page is the one that is listed in search engines and displayed on all the church's printed materials.

I think a church has two choices. If the church's news must go on the home page, keep it to headlines only. Then, in a prominent place, give additional links for those who may be new to the church. Perhaps there could be news headlines down the right-hand side, while the visually more important left-hand side (as this is where the eye starts as it reads from left to right) could contain links such as 'Getting married in St Mark's' and 'George Gilbert Scott's wonderful Victorian building.'

Alternatively, the news items for the congregation can be relegated to subpages. The home page can be left entirely for those who are unfamiliar with the church. One church web site I know of has three clear visitor's links from the home page—one for visitors who live in the local community, one for people in the UK (they could be visiting the area or moving house) and one for overseas visitors which links to information about the town.

Why do churches use welcoming teams on their doors? Is it not to spot newcomers and to make them feel at home? In the same way, the church's home page needs to earn its name and feel like *home* for those unsure of what they are looking for and uncertain of the welcome they will receive.

4
Creating Your Church Web Site

Starting point

The starting point in creating your own church web site must be to think about your possible audience. The question to ask is why new people might come to the church and then design your site to encourage this to happen. Do you have an active under-fives group which attracts young parents? Is your church in demand for weddings? If so, these are the issues which need to be on your site. In due course new people may appreciate the minister's sermons, but that is probably not their immediate need.

In the introduction I referred to Dora Bletchley. It is worth creating half a dozen or so such characters. Give them names and short descriptions. Do they live in terraced housing? how old are they? how might the church help them? and so on. As you discuss your site, you can create content for these people. You will find yourself saying, 'that's OK for Dora, but Sally wouldn't understand that.' The St Mark's Church site looked at in the previous section does not work for its intended audience because they took material—the Welcome Pack—that is given to newcomers to church services. Someone who comes to a service can be very different from someone browsing your web site for information.

The *Yale Web Style Guide* (**http://info.med.yale.edu/caim/manual/index.html)** puts it like this:

> The first step in designing a web site is to make sure you have defined a set of goals—know what it is you want to accomplish with your web site. Without a clear statement of purpose and objectives the project will begin to wander off course and bog down, or may go on past the point of diminishing returns. Careful planning and a clear sense of purpose are the keys to success in building web sites, particularly if you will be working as part of a team to build the site. Before beginning to build your web site you should:
>
> - Identify your target audience
> - Have a statement of purpose
> - Know your main objectives
> - Have a concise outline of the information your site will contain.'

The excellent article on web evangelism at **http://www.brigada.org** also suggests:

> We humbly suggest it is not often wise to mix material which is intended primarily for Christians with that which is evangelistic. If a site is designed to be aimed at Christians, to tell them about your ministry, mission, or church, that is fine. But if you want material to be evangelistic, *keep it quite separate*

from any material designed for believers. The situation is completely different from preaching a sermon in a guest service, where the speaker may well at one time be speaking mainly to the Christians present, and yet in the next breath be addressing the non-Christians. On the web, you are not speaking to a captive group, but an individual.

A Dangerous Perspective

There is a real danger that we see the production of a web site as *publishing*. The software you use may even employ this term for the final stage of moving pages from your computer to the internet. But it is a dangerous word as it conveys the production of texts and images that others passively view. The web is much, much more. Your site should be about establishing a relationship with at least some of the site's visitors.

Web site designers talk of visitors and never readers. If someone were to visit your church building in person, you hope they would be more than a passive observer. You would want to welcome them, talk with them, introduce them to others, invite them to sign a visitor's book, maybe follow-up their visit by a call. These are all important words: visit, welcome, talk, introduce, invite, sign, call. This is not publishing but starting a *relationship*.

In creating your church web site, how do you describe your task? Is it merely informing Dora Bletchley of the time of the Family Service, or is it to invite her to attend? Is it merely to tell James and Sally that weddings take place between 10 and 4 or to forge a link with a couple who see your church (and maybe your God) as part of their marriage? I suggest that against every 'Dora' you create you jot down your objective using some of the words from this section. How are you going to establish a relationship with your *visitors*?

This change of perspective—from publishing to relationship building—will change the way you design your site.

The Team

Wherever possible, creating a church web site should be a team affair. The computer enthusiast who knows how to publish pages to a web server may not be the right person to write the content. The minister—long trained in writing essays and delivering sermons—may not be the best person to submit magazine-style articles. What would make a good team?

- Someone who can write short, jargon-free articles.
- Someone who has an eye for layout, colours and design.
- Someone who can act as overall editor, preferably with some theological awareness and pastoral sensitivity.
- Someone who can assemble the pages and publish them on to the web.
- Someone with spare time to submit the details of the site to the various search engines and directories and ensure that the church's web address is known in the community.

- Someone to update the content regularly if you have a site with news and event information.
- Someone to communicate the aims—and progress—of the site to the wider church and to encourage prayer for its effectiveness.

A team of seven is a very tall order in most churches! All these tasks may get rolled into one or two people. But in talking of a team, the point is that there are a variety of things to be done. This is not the sole domain of a computer enthusiast.

It is worth remembering that young people often have more skills—and certainly more enthusiasm—for this medium than many older people. Draft one or two young people into the team. This is one area in the church where they can help. A couple of decades ago churches could retain their young men by putting them in an (all-male) choir or asking them to serve at Holy Communion. Less so today. But the web is one area of church work which may fire their imagination. Get them involved, for their sakes as well as the church's.

Helping to building a web site may also be a worthwhile ministry for those less able to serve in other ways. For once, being housebound is an advantage!

Another approach to working as a team is to gather the necessary skills—and perhaps budget—as an ecumenical project. People outside of the church are not interested in our doctrinal differences and variations in worship. A united web site is a witness in itself. Furthermore, as a churches-in-the-community site it may be more helpful for outsiders in the same way that a restaurant guide is easier to consult than half-a-dozen restaurant pub sites.

Content
What type of material works well on the web?
- Because the present focus of the web is for information, people will look to a church's web site for facts about the church and its life. When is the next parade service, how can I get married in the church, what is the history of the building?
- Because the style of the web is more magazine than book, the content will be small pieces of text. The church members may read the vicar's sermons posted on the church site, but do not expect anyone else to. However, a short explanation of what it means to be a Christian today could be used.
- Because the approach of the web is non-authoritarian, the church's site is just its own perspective on life. Your beliefs are just as valid as anyone else's but not more so. So personal testimonies and explorations of the journey of faith along the lines of 'this is our story, tell us yours' will be more acceptable than convincing people that Jesus is the Son of God. A church in Texas has a group photograph of a dozen church members on its home page. Clicking on each individual brings up his or her testimony. Young people can click on the teenagers, older people on the retired couple. See **http://www.lufkinfirst assembly.org**. It works very well as it introduces both church and personal faith from a variety of perspectives.

15

- Because the nature of the web is to allow responses, people will not be offended if responses are invited via comment forms and guest books. They can ignore them if they wish just as they can ignore the visitor's book at the back of church. People are wary of their e-mail address being used for unwanted junk mail, so care needs to be taken in collecting personal details.

There is simply not sufficient space in this short booklet to go into how to write for the web. There are the usual warnings that go with any evangelistic endeavour. Ban jargon, relate to your audience, keep it short and simple. There are also a few techniques special to this medium such as using clear navigation, inviting responses via forms and linking to other sites with relevant material. On **http://www.webevangelism.net** there are some more detailed pointers and **http://www.brigada.org** offers lots of useful advice.

DIY Software

A discussion on the many software tools available is also another book. Which web page editor is best? Internet magazines run reviews of web site design software and are a good place to look for up-to-date advice.

Not surprisingly, the best tool is the one most suited to the job, and this depends on the size and complexity of the site you are building. For a site of only a handful of pages almost any tool will do. To my mind it comes down to how easy it is for you to use. Do you have to understand HTML—the language of the web—or simply type in your content much as you would with a word processor?

Perhaps more importantly, does the software include page designs that you can use? That is, are there pre-designed buttons and colour schemes you can employ? In creating a web site you are not only creating content but also a design, and this is where many sites fall down.

If you need to develop a large site with scores or even hundreds of pages, you will also need to look at software with good site tools. These allow you to move pages around without losing the navigation links between the pages.

Employing a Designer

You can ask a web designer to build your site for you. A designer will charge but the advantage is that you will end up with a good-looking site. The big disadvantage is that since someone else built it, updating the content may be more difficult. You may not need to change the content from one month to the next if the site is a 'brochure' site that only describes the facilities of the church. But if it is a magazine site where the content needs to change at least monthly, updating it can be a problem as most churches will not be able to afford to return again and again to the designers.

You can mix the designer and the DIY approach. You could ask a designer to create some templates for you to work with or even just design the graphics. Then, using your own software, you could add the content. Be willing, very willing, to sacrifice complex design in favour of easy updating.

Using a Database

You may decide to create a site which has news items and lists of events. But who is going to update these on a regular basis? If different people frequently want to update a diary page, there will be a bottleneck if everything has to go through one designer. Time after time, church sites languish once the initial enthusiasm has faded and the regular chore of updating begins.

The solution is an on-line database. A range of people will be able to contribute items (such as articles, event notifications and news items) by simply entering them into an on-line form. A database designed to show news items would have an administration form (only available by keying in a password, of course) which has boxes to fill in for the name, date and details of the item. Clicking on the *add* button would add the item to the database, which in turn would automatically update your news page to display it. See **www.webevangelism.net** for some further pointers.

5
The 'Virtual Church Hall'

In the past churches and their church halls have been focal points for local communities. Often the village or parish hall was built next to the church and administered by the church. Within its walls met all sorts of groups. Some were church groups but others were just grateful for a home for their meetings. So the local dramatics society occupied the building on Mondays, the WI on Tuesdays and the church youth club on Wednesdays, and so on throughout the week. The church was at the heart of the community. Its relationship with some of the hall's occupants may have been limited, or simply commercial. With others the link was stronger and the borders between church and non-church more hazy. By virtue of its church hall, the church acted at the centre of community life and was able to touch many who never came to Sunday services.

In a similar way, the church might consider building a 'virtual church hall.' The church could be in a position to take the initiative or chair in developing a local community web site. Societies and clubs in the village/area could be given a page of web space to describe themselves. There could be a central database of events and news. There could be links to external information, such as county and council sites, relevant search engines and national news. Its aim would be to provide a hub of community information.

If the church plays an important role in the site's creation, it will be natural to see the site reflect church content. This content need not be tucked away on the church's own site, but be part of the community material—much as some radio stations include a spiritual thought for the day before their news bulletins. As such a community site is built, develops and is regularly updated, church members will join with others in working for the community. The witness of these individuals as well as the church's community focus will add authenticity to the gospel content of the church's web material.

By means of a virtual church hall, the church can express its concern for the community. It can be embracing rather than reclusive. It can present a spiritual message in the midst of ordinary daily life.

Building a Virtual Church Hall

Building such a site requires more than a simple 3-page web site. If news items are to be contributed by many, then the site will need a way of allowing entries typed into a form to be added to the home page as headlines and linked to a page of further details. This either calls for an enthusiastic team with loads of time to update the site at least weekly or it requires pages driven by a database.

Many of the national sites which hold maps, timetables, cinema listings and the like are happy to see their material displayed as part of your web site. They usually insist that their logo is displayed (with a full link to their site) or they may want to include advertising. As a community site you may feel more open to displaying advertising sourced from local shops and firms.

Taking on this sort of venture is not a small step. Alongside the technological questions are the human and political ones associated with community life. But the very act of working with the community will pay dividends.

Town Sites

The business opportunities for community sites in towns have not gone unnoticed! Just as local papers offer a viable business, so a well-run community site can attract sufficient hits to make local advertising pay its way. A number of town sites belong to larger organizations—again in similar way that a larger parent group often owns local newspapers.

Often these town sites are crying out for—no, desperate for—content for their pages. The news items of the local church, even the articles of the parish magazine, can all provide useful content. The local church can become a main contributor or leading voice within the site. And where the town is larger, it may be better to work together as an ecumenical group to provide content.

Create Content, Not Just a Church Site

The web gets its name for a reason. Not only does it present a labyrinth of cross-referenced pages, but it allows pages from one site to be used and displayed in another site. A community site can go further than just adding a link to your church site. They can take the pages you have created for your site and display them as part of theirs.

This is a significant change of focus. Instead of building only a church site you are creating *content* to be used on other sites as well. When people ask me about getting their church on to the web they invariable think only in terms of their own web site. That their pages can be easily included on other people's sites comes as a surprise. So before you design your church site, take a look at your local community sites. It may be that if you present your content (such as your church's history or your list of services) in a particular way, the community site will include it too.

Fruitless Searching

Many people find search engines frustrating. The item they are looking for is buried in hundreds of unwanted references. As the number of pages on the web expands dramatically, this frustration will only increase. One effect is that people are turning from some of the global and national sites to more local ones. Why waste time on national cinema listings when your own town site has the information you need? Why wade through the national business directories when you can find a plumber on the town site?

In this way the local sites may become more important as the web gets ever bigger. It is therefore all the more important that local churches are well represented.

6
Linking to National Resources

Many, many churches around the world have run *Alpha* courses. Local churches have benefited from a national resource—through the ideas and materials from a professionally produced course.

Local to National

In the same way a local church web site ought to be able to draw on national resources for mission. Rather than write an explanation of the gospel themselves, local church web designers could link to other, national sites which can do it more effectively and professionally. If such national sites were truly set up as resources, the pages could be incorporated into the local church site without additional 'branding' getting in the way to confuse the surfer.

National to Local

The flow need not always be from the local to the national. It ought to go the other way as well. When Billy Graham brought his missions to town, he would only come if the local churches were fully involved. He realized that those who came forward would need follow-up and nurture. So all the details taken of enquirers were forwarded to local churches. In the same way, a national web site that promotes an understanding of the Christian faith could refer people to local churches, either by including a local church search facility or by passing on messages left on the site to registered churches.

Four Case Studies

So where are these valuable national sites? A few exist—of variable quality—but they are certainly not there in abundance. This may be because the vision has not been grasped. It may be because there is no recognized way of funding such an enterprise.

Below are four web sites that could be used as resources for your own web site. They are listed here merely as examples of different approaches. Looking at these could start a useful discussion for those for a group planning a site. What do these sites get right? What is suitable for your church? There are others listed at **http://www.webevangelism.net.**

Church of England   http://www.church-of-england.org

From the home page of the Church of England site you can look at sections which talk about baptism, marriage and funerals. These could be just the sort of pages to which a local Anglican church might link to refer those coming to their sites with questions in these areas.

Take a look for yourself to judge their suitability for your use. They seek to draw the reader's interest into the wider issues of belief, although the marriage page gets quickly embroiled in the legalities of who can marry whom and where. There is important legal, practical and pastoral advice on these pages, though I suspect many would want more evangelism.

The site also attempts to relate people back to local churches though a sister site called **http://www.church-search.com.** This allows people to search for a church in their neighbourhood, whether they have a web site or not.

Power to Change   http://www.powertochange.com

Power to Change is a site based in Canada. It features a number of well-designed pages on 'questions of life' and Christian belief. Its strongest area is the extensive collection of personal testimonies. Inevitably, these have a North American bias, but some testimonies are from sports people known all over the world. Mixed among the famous are stories of 'ordinary people' which could work well in other cultures.

The American feel may not be suitable for Europeans. But the site is an excellent example of how personal testimonies can work on the web. If this is not suitable to link to, then it is worth learning from.

Baptist.org   http://www.baptist.org

A Southern Baptist site has a link on its home page to **http://www.baptist.org/ GoToHeaven/HowToComeToGod.htm** (and even the choice of folder and file names raises an issue!). This link opens up a new browser window for a gospel presentation. The page stands by itself (there are no links to the Baptist.org site) so could be called from anywhere. The page presents the gospel through images and Bible verses, all with a background of music.

At the bottom of the page is a button inviting you to accept Christ. Clicking this brings up a response page, accompanied by music for the hymn *Just as I am*! Any response you enter into the form goes back to the author, which means that this page is not helpful for use by other churches. Having an easy-to-use response form is good, but the site reflects the media of tracts and altar calls. Look for yourself and assess whether or not this works on the internet.

Deeper Still   http://www.grieving.org

The International Bible Society has a special site which offers pages on how the Bible helps those who are grieving. It is written to be accessible to non-Christians, sensitively showing that God is there for everyone at such times of crisis. The pages include a comprehensive set of links to other grief and related resources.

This is the kind of site that can be of real benefit to local church sites which link to it. The site (with an excellent domain name) meets a general need yet weaves in Christian spirituality as it does so.

Other Resources

In order to create interactive sites with the ability for users to respond, churches include items such as guest books. Some will add events calendars, news lists and even discussion and chat areas. These sorts of applications require programming and are beyond the skill of most churches. However, you can run these applications on someone else's computer and merely link to them from your site.

The web has many places where you can go to get these resources for free. So you can sign up with a guest book supplier (such as **http://www.beseen.com**) who allows you to run your own guest book on their servers for free. They handle all the complicated design and programming; you just make a link from your site to theirs. So where is the catch?

The majority of these sites need to make an income somehow. Their free offerings come with the requirement that they can display adverts on the pages they provide. This can really jar as promotions for life insurance get displayed above a prayer request form! However, not all of these service sites demand advertising. They may only ask you to display their logo on your pages. Still be cautious. If the link is good (say to a national or global news service), people may get hooked into the linked site (after all, that is their aim) and they will be lost to you.

The alternative is to pay for the service, and some of these sites offer an advert-free service in return for an annual fee. Alternatively, Christian internet service providers may be able to offer suitable services without inappropriate advertising.

7
Making Your Site Known

If you have a site that is designed to be useful and attractive for those outside the church, you have to ensure they can find it. A couple may be moving into your area and decide to look up the local church. A young mother may be looking for under fives groups. How do they find your site and, through it, your church?

Get a Good Name

The domain name is a web address that can be used both for web access and for e-mail. So, a church in Taunton might register the domain name stmarys-taunton.org.uk, which would mean that their web site would be at **www.stmarys-taunton.org.uk** and they could use e-mail addresses such as **vicar@stmarys-taunton.org.uk** and **underfives@stmarys-taunton.org.uk**.

The advantage of registering your own domain is that it is more memorable. The simpler names such as stmarys.org.uk may well have been snapped up years ago, but including the town or village name will distinguish you from other, similarly-named churches and will give you a slight advantage in search engines.

More can be said about the technicalities, but this has been left to **www.web evangelism.net**. There is one last important fact. Buying a domain name is cheap these days. Every church should have one, even if they do not immediately use it.

Using Your Domain

To find your site, people will use search engines. These special web sites scour the web indexing pages they find so that someone entering a phrase such as 'churches in Taunton' has a chance of finding a reference to your site. There are also web directories, which allow you to enter your site into certain categories. They may, for example, have a list of churches divided into geographical areas. Alongside the general search engines and directories are their Christian equivalents which only list religious sites.

Submitting your site to the various search engines on the web is important. But far more important is making your domain name known in the local community through your existing publicity channels. Emblazon your church magazine with your domain name, paint it on your church notice board, print it on all your letterheads. Wherever your church name is mentioned, make sure the domain name is given too. So choose wisely in registering a domain name. It is not something you want to change every year or so!

Search Engines

The larger search engines may well, eventually, find your site even if you do nothing. But you should not leave it to chance. You should submit the details of your church site so that they can know where to look. Once they have your submission, the search engine will scan your pages and create cross-references to it in its vast database of sites. Be patient. Following the submission of your details, this can take weeks to happen.

There are four sets of search engines/directories you should consider:

- The large, global search engines such as AltaVista, Lycos, Google and Excite.
- The country-specific versions of the global engines, such as excite.co.uk as well as excite.com.
- Christian directories, both national and world-wide.
- Local community directories.

You can find further details on search engines, both general and Christian, in my book *God on the Net* (HarperCollins). Getting to the number one slot in one of the top search engines is an exacting and expensive task, way beyond the resources of a local church. However, it is important to submit your site to the main search engines. You may not be the number one site listed when people search for 'Christian,' but you will be found if someone is searching more specifically for 'churches in Taunton.'

Perhaps more important than the global and national search engines and directories are the sites which cover your local community.

- Has your town got its own community site?
- Does the town or county council run a site listing local amenities?
- Are there sites to help tourists in the area?

Make sure your church is listed. As the web becomes ever larger, the information people want to find will become ever more elusive. People on the web will turn away from the world-wide bit and look to their local sites to provide information. What good is a list of 10,000 plumbers world-wide when a person wants someone who can mend their leaking taps? Similarly, a mother will want their young infant to go to a toddler group in her own town, in Taunton not Toronto.

Hard Work

I do not know of any effective short cuts here. Finding the local sites in which you want a link will take time. Submitting to the large search engines also takes time. On the brighter side, it does not require knowledge of HTML (the programming language of web pages) nor design skills, only the patience to track down the important sites and fill in their submission forms. It is an ideal job for a retired or housebound person.

Do not expect wonders from the search engines. You will not be overwhelmed with casual surfers. Pay more attention to your existing publicity routes and add your domain name to anything that is printed or displayed. St Mark's Church (see the earlier section) may have a web site but its church notice board, seen by hundreds in the community, makes no mention of it. It is an opportunity missed.

8
Summary

What are my seven most important points when summarizing church web sites and evangelism?

1. Get it in perspective. The web site is only a support and resource.
2. Focus your web site on the people who will visit it and on their questions. Make the first page a true 'home' for those outside the church.
3. Recognize that the web medium is different from other media such as books, services and the church magazine. Think in terms of meeting visitors and not publishing material.
4. Build the site as a team if you can. Enlist young people.
5. Remember that the pages you create might be usable in other neighbourhood sites.
6. Think about a virtual church hall or at least building your site as an ecumenical project.
7. Get your own domain name. Plaster it on all your publicity and regularly submit your site to search engines and community directories.